THE TABLETOP LEARNING SERIES

RAINY DAY

Magic for Wonderful Wet Weather

by Imogene Forte

Incentive Publications, Inc.
Nashville, Tennessee

Illustrated by Becky Cutler
Cover designed by Mary Hamilton and illustrated by Jan Cunningham
Edited by Susan Oglander

Library of Congress Catalog Number 83-82332
ISBN 0-86530-094-1

THIS
RAINY DAY BOOK
BELONGS TO

_____

CONTENTS

I WONDER WHY?

RAIN, RAIN DON'T GO AWAY — WE WANT TO PLAY!

Rainy days are much too special to waste waiting and wishing for the sun to shine. This book was written to help you ...

- ... experience the magic of raindrops falling on your head on a warm summer day
- ... sense the excitement of exploring a newly created puddle
- ... shiver to the ooze of squishy mud between your fingers and toes
- ... thrill to the colors of the rainbow right under your nose
- ... be amazed by raindrops racing down your windowpane on a dreary day
- ... construct clouds and dams, sail puddle boats, conduct weather experiments, and find answers to your own rainy day questions.

Begin NOW to organize your supplies and equipment so that you are ready to enjoy the next rainy day from beginning to end. If you wait until the sound of the first raindrop on the roof to begin looking for the things you will need, you will still be searching when the rain is over, especially if it is a sudden spring shower or an unexpected winter storm. Who knows how many rainbows you might miss this way?

The first page in each section tells you how to organize your supplies so you will be ready at a moment's notice for wet weather projects, indoor activities, and rainy day research. You can find nearly all the things you need around the house so you don't have to go shopping or searching to set up your rainy day lab for learning.

So, come, get set to get wet, to enjoy being high and dry, to wonder why and to make your own rainbow on the very next rainy day.

Imogene Forte

GET SET TO GET WET

things to do outside

PICK UP AND GO PAIL

to get set to get wet

Find yourself a good-sized plastic pail with a handle to hold the supplies you will need to be all "set to get wet" the next time it rains. A scrub pail or sand bucket would work nicely.

Into your pail go ...

> ... a collection of spoons and forks (old ones, of course, that you have permission to use)
> ... an old comb and brush (to make the nicest curves and curlicues in mud)
> ... funnels, sifters, and scoops
> ... measuring cups and glass jars with lids
> ... plastic squeeze bottles and a bleach or milk jug
> ... sponges and an old towel for cleanup
> ... a magnifying glass if you have one

Add anything else that you think you will really need. Do be careful, however, not to just pitch in any old thing. Rainy days are much too special to be wasted sorting through a lot of junk and clutter.

12

ARTIST AT WORK

with mud of all things

You can't hang this art in a museum, or even save it for yourself, but it is sure to be fun while you are creating it.

Find a stretch of sidewalk near a puddle full of nice squishy mud, have several brushes of different sizes handy (paint brushes, scrub brushes, hair brushes, vegetable brushes, and toothbrushes are great), and get to work on your masterpiece.

You may plan your picture before you begin and try to make it very "real" looking, or maybe you will want to just make lines and shapes and let the mud make its own design. The idea is to have fun with the mud and enjoy the results.

Be sure to wash it all away with big pails of water after you have shared your mud masterpiece with your friends.

MAKE A MUD MONSTER

better than a snowman

After a rain, use your hands to gather up a big mound of mud. Then begin to fashion balls just as if you were going to make a snowman. If the mud is too squishy to hold together, find some drier dirt under a big leafy tree or somewhere where it didn't get quite so wet. (A bit of sawdust is really great for this if you happen to have it.) Mix the dry dirt into the mud until it is stiff enough to shape with your hands.

Dream up the craziest or funniest-looking monster you can and get to work. You may want to use a sand shovel or a big kitchen spoon to help shape your monster. Use pebbles, twigs, slivers of wood or anything you can find for eyes, ears, nose, mouth and any other features. Give your monster a name and let him dry in the sun. This is a lot of fun to do with other kids because mud monsters like lots of company.

Note
Of course you will want to wear old clothes and shoes (or no shoes if it's a warm day) when you tackle this monstrous project. No need spoiling a good outfit or making life hard for the person who washes your clothes.

ADD ONE MORE RAINBOW

made by you and the rain

You will need a box top large enough to hold a sheet of drawing paper and sturdy enough to be left in the rain for a bit, red, blue, and yellow tempera or poster paints, a paintbrush, and the drawing paper.

Using the three colors, paint a rainbow on the paper. Try to paint the stripes so that your finished painting will have all seven of the rainbow's colors (red, orange, yellow, green, blue, indigo, and violet). You can do this if you work carefully because the three colors you are using are the basic primary colors from which the others are made. Blue and yellow make green, red and yellow make orange, blue and red make violet, and blue and violet make indigo.

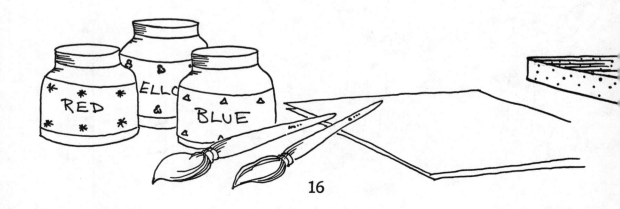

When you have finished painting your rainbow, place it carefully inside the box top (if you don't have a box top, a large tray will do) and put it out in the rain for a few minutes. The rain should cause the colors to flow together and blend just enough to give you a more natural-looking rainbow.

Bring your rainbow inside to dry, and then hang it on the wall in your room. Or, you could paste your rainbow on the top of a box to hold a special collection or a gift for a friend. Whoever said you can't "hang on to a rainbow" and save it for another day?

A BIT OF MUD MADNESS

to bring out the creative side of you

Go outside right after the rain stops and find a nice muddy spot to set up your mud studio. You will need a big piece of corrugated cardboard (one side of a good sturdy box would work nicely) and some sticks, spoons, forks, or an old comb and brush.

Use your hands to make a big pile of squishy mud to work with. Spoon some of the mud onto the center of the cardboard. Begin to spread it on the board just as you would finger paint. Then use your palms, fists, fingers, wrists and elbows, forks, spoons, the comb and brush or anything else you think of to give depth and motion to your creation. Keep adding mud as you need it to finish your design.

Look around for pebbles, bits of wood or bark, leaves or twigs, bird feathers, or dead insects left behind by the rain or floating on nearby puddles. Select some of these to press into your "mud madness" to add interest. Place the finished work in the sun to dry.

19

MAKE YOUR OWN RAINBOW

all it takes is the right angle

If you have waited and waited, and still have not seen a rainbow, don't despair. Get a grownup you like to help you make one of your own.

Ask the grownup to spray a fine mist from a garden hose in front of you while you stand with your back to the sun. If you look directly into the spray at a 45 degree angle, you should see the colors of the rainbow. (Ask the grownup to help you with the 45 degree angle bit.) It is tricky and may take some work, but you will be enjoying the sunny outdoors while you search for your own rainbow.

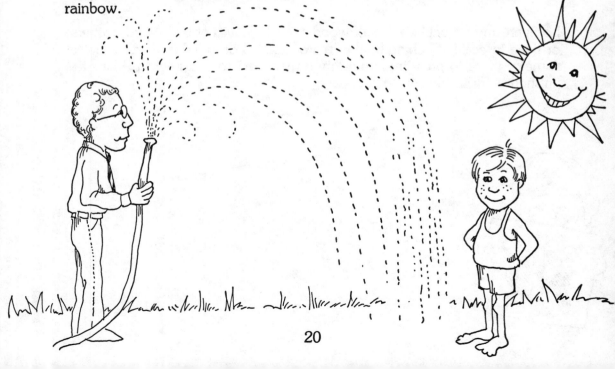

RAINY DAY SHELTER

stay dry and watch it rain

This activity is for warm summer rains. You will need an old rain poncho or a vinyl tablecloth, and a golf or beach umbrella. Select a cozy spot outside . . . perhaps a favorite thinking place. Tilt your umbrella over on its side, cover it with the poncho or tablecloth, then crawl into your shelter and cuddle up to enjoy watching the raindrops fall. If you happen to have a large leafy tree or an evergreen tree nearby, you might use it instead for your special rainy day hideaway. (This is a rainy day project — not a stormy day one!)

STUDY THE SKY

to be weather wise

Long before modern scientific methods of observing and forecasting the weather were developed, people had to study the weather as best they could. Farmers, fishermen, sailors, and others who depended on the soil or the sea for their livelihood became pretty good at this. Almost every village had someone who was considered "weather wise" because he could predict the weather.

Many old sayings grew out of the study of the sky. What do you think these sayings meant?

"Red sky at night, sailor's delight,"
"Red sky in the morning, sailor take
    warning."

"Swallows flying high mean no rain in the
    sky,"
"Swallows near the ground mean rain will
    come around."

A meteorologist is trained to study the weather with the help of photographs from satellites and other modern scientific equipment. Even though you might not be a trained meteorologist, you can begin to become "weather wise" by taking a trip outside and learning to observe the wind and the clouds.

BE A BUSY BEAVER

build a dam

Mound up a lot of sticks, stones, and mud to build a dam to reroute the water's flow right after a heavy rain. Build small foil boats to float on the water's surface. Try loading the boats with small twigs and leaves to see how much weight they can carry and what happens when they become over-loaded. When you have finished observing the water, tear your dam apart and let the water run free. What does this teach you about flood control?

SET SAIL IN A PUDDLE

you'll be amazed at your floating boat

Build a special sailboat to float in the puddle of your choice.

In a big puddle you could use a piece of bark or Styrofoam.

For a middle-sized puddle try soap that floats or a sponge.

For a tiny puddle you might choose
a walnut shell half or a bottle cap.

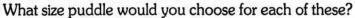

What size puddle would you choose for each of these?
- an aluminum pie plate
- a plastic cereal bowl or saucer
- a hair brush or scrub brush

(You can add a cloth or paper sail to any of them,
of course.)

Wouldn't it be fun to ask a friend or two
to join you for a floating boat race?

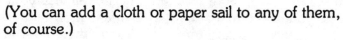

WHO GOES THERE?

these muddy footprints will never tell

Gather up a collection of old shoes and socks and go in search of a nice long stretch of good, squishy mud. Then, begin to make different kinds of footprints in the mud.

Put on a tennis shoe, a rubber thong sandal, the shoe belonging to the biggest foot in your house, a lady's high heel, a rubber boot, an old sock of your own, a lady's nylon, or a sock with some of the toes cut out. Just for fun, try an old mitten on your foot, and, best of all, use your own bare feet. As you press your feet into the mud, try to make monster tracks, giant tracks, gnome tracks, space creature tracks, and any others your imagination suggests.

Sit back and look at the tracks you left in the mud and select some to make up a story about. This is a fun thing for two people or a group to do together because the tales get taller and taller when there is an audience.

_____

_____

_____

_____

_____

_____

_____

_____

_____

_____

_____

_____

HIGH AND DRY

things to do inside

RAINBOW MAKER'S TOOL TOTE

for when you are high and dry

Have you ever searched and searched for your paintbrushes and paints, looked everywhere for your scissors, or found the red crayon missing from the box just when you needed it?

To avoid having these things happen, make a tool tote to hold all your gear. You will need a cardboard soft drink carton, some paste and paper to cover and decorate it, and scissors.

Cut the paper to fit the carton and paste it on. Select your favorite colors, and take the time to cut out some cheerful decorations. This tote will last a long time and will serve you well, so you want it to be special.

Fill the tote with the tools of your trade: rulers, scissors, pencils, crayons, felt tip pens, paste, paints and brushes, yarn, and string. Store the tote in a big plastic bag with a pad of drawing paper, a pack of colored construction paper, a roll of clear plastic wrap, and some tissue paper.

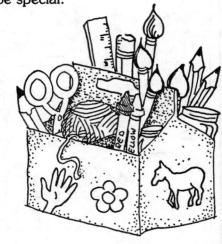

Your rainbow maker's tote will be ready for the next rainy day at a moment's notice!

TEAR A RAINY DAY SCENE

scissors not allowed

Rain on the green grass
And rain on the tree,
Rain on the rooftop,
But not on me!

Make a torn-paper collage to illustrate this nursery rhyme. Test your creative ability by using manila paper for the background, and only three colors of construction paper for your design. Choose your colors carefully and plan your entire illustration before you begin tearing. Tear the figures you want to use and paste them on the background paper for a design that shows you as the only dry thing in the scene.

RAINMAKER, RAINMAKER, CAN YOU MAKE IT RAIN?

it might start coming down!

Throughout history, people have used all kinds of different methods to try to make it rain. Primitive tribes of old had rainmakers with bags of special tricks, and some rainmakers traveled from village to village with colorful rituals and secret potions. Many tall tales have been told of these rainmakers and their adventures.

In more recent times, scientists have used chemicals to set off rainfall. These chemicals are released by pilots who fly among the clouds. Some of these methods have been more successful than others, but man has still not been able to gain control of the weather.

Find out what really causes rain.

DANCE A RAIN DANCE

heel and toe, heel and toe, make it up as you go

One of the most colorful methods used to try to make it rain is the rain dance. Many North American Indians had their own tribal rain dance and it is said that members of one brave Indian tribe danced with rattlesnakes in their mouths. Other are reported to have used different types of ceremonial dances to encourage the powers controlling the rain to show favor on them. We read that these dances were very colorful and lively.

Make up your own rain dance, with or without words, then ask your friends to dance with you.

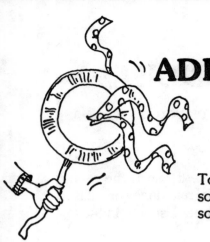

ADD A DASH OF RHYTHM

listen for the sound of raindrops

To add extra excitement to your rain dance, ask some friends to join you in making and playing some of these rhythm instruments.

Put a handful of small pebbles between two aluminum pie tins. Use a ruler or stick for a handle and tape the plates together with masking tape. Paste on some tissue paper streamers to add color to your "rainmaker's magic shaker."

Fill two empty plastic detergent bottles about half full of beans. Fasten on the tops securely, and tie on long pieces of brightly colored yarn to float in the breeze as you shake, rattle, and roll the rhythm bottles — one in each hand!

Put a big spoonful of rice or small pieces of macaroni in each of two small boxes. Tape the boxes shut. Glue sandpaper to one side of both the boxes. Use your felt tip pens to make rainbows on the "rub-a-dub-dub cubes."

Completely cover two light blubs with several layers of newspaper strips dipped in homemade flour paste (flour and water). Let the paste dry, then use felt tip pens to draw on rainmaker's magic marks. Carefully tap the bulbs on the edge of a table to break the inside. You will have perfect maracas for a rain dance.

Paint rainmaker voodoo signs on an old tin pan with a handle. Search through the drawers for just the right forks or spoons to make the "tap, tap, rap, rap, make-the-rain-come rhythms" you want.

Tie a metal door hook or kitchen grater to a string. Use a nail to clink, clank, plink, plank your plea for rain.

To complete your rainy rhythm section, two tin pan tops will make great rain dance cymbals.

RAINY DAY SCRIBBLE

finish it in a fantastic fashion

It's raining, it's pouring,
The old man is snoring.
He went to bed with a cold in his head
And he didn't wake up until morning.

Lay a piece of tracing paper over the scribbles on the next page. Then add lines to the scribbles to make a drawing to illustrate the nursery rhyme. Use your crayons to color the picture and give it to someone you like as a rainy day surprise.

Note
The next time it rains, try making some unfinished scribbles of your own for someone else to finish.

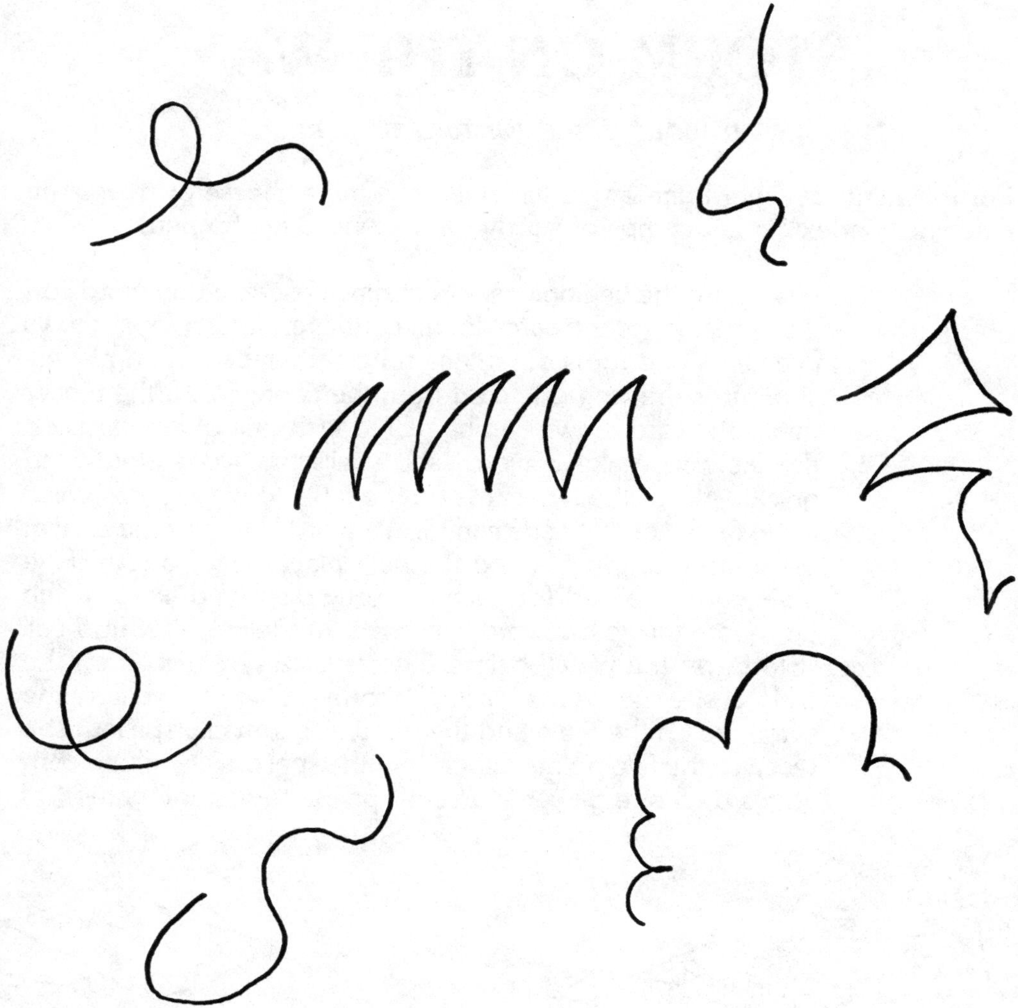

STORM ON THE WAY

a word game for two players

For this rainy day word game you will need a cottage cheese or margarine container, index cards or strips of sturdy paper, and a felt tip pen.

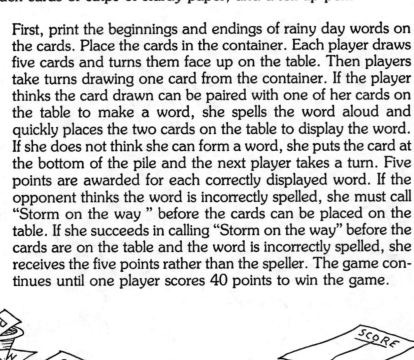

First, print the beginnings and endings of rainy day words on the cards. Place the cards in the container. Each player draws five cards and turns them face up on the table. Then players take turns drawing one card from the container. If the player thinks the card drawn can be paired with one of her cards on the table to make a word, she spells the word aloud and quickly places the two cards on the table to display the word. If she does not think she can form a word, she puts the card at the bottom of the pile and the next player takes a turn. Five points are awarded for each correctly displayed word. If the opponent thinks the word is incorrectly spelled, she must call "Storm on the way" before the cards can be placed on the table. If she succeeds in calling "Storm on the way" before the cards are on the table and the word is incorrectly spelled, she receives the five points rather than the speller. The game continues until one player scores 40 points to win the game.

Here are some word beginnings and endings to help you get started. (Some are whole words, but must be paired with either a beginning or an ending to make a new word. For example, you may want to include more than one card with *rain, y, ing,* and *ed* in order to provide more choices.)

rain/storm
light/ning
thun/der/storm
pud/dle
cloud/y
um/brella
splash/ing

slick/er
drip/drop
down/pour
weath/er
show/er
soak/ed
rain/bow

STORY'S END

two endings are better than one

Select one of these titles for a rainy day story. Write your story, and then read all of it except the end to a friend. Ask your friend to furnish an ending, and compare his "story's end" with yours.

The Day It Rained Chocolate Pudding
After the Flood
The Girl with the Magic Umbrella
The Case of the Missing Raincoat
Pete the Puddle Jumper
The Rainy Day Mystery
Waco the Weatherman's Most Serious Mistake
Belinda and the Bewitched Umbrella
Rainbows For Sale
Found! Two Wet Kittens

WET WEATHER SEARCH

a cut and paste game

All you will need to play this game is a stack of old magazines, paper, an alarm clock, scissors, paste, and a friend.

Divide the magazines evenly so that each of you has the same number. Set the alarm clock for a specified amount of time such as five or ten minutes. Then, begin looking for pictures of rainy day scenes in the magazines. The person who finds, cuts out, and pastes the most scenes on his paper is the winner. You must move quickly because only pasted scenes count.

41

I WISH, I WISH, I WISH . . .

what do I do to make it come true?

Just pretend that someone walks into your room on a misty, moist morning and gives you a magic umbrella. Tied on to the umbrella is a note saying:

Sit under this umbrella
And make three wishes,
One wish for your family
One for your country,
And one for you!
Think about it
And wish very carefully,
Because each of these wishes
Will come true.

. . . UPON A MAGIC UMBRELLA

Write each wish on a separate sheet of paper.

More than anything in the world, I wish that my family . . . .
I wish that my country . . . .
And for me, I wish . . . .

When you have written all three
wishes, turn your paper over and
write what effect you think each of
these wishes will have. Will your
family, your country, or you really
be happier, healthier, or stronger
because of the wish? Will the
results be long lasting or just fun
for a day or two?

Wishing is serious business, isn't it?

SUPER SCOOP

pick up a whole new world

Make this handy scoop for all sorts of rainy day activities. All you need are some strong scissors and a plastic bottle or jug that once held milk, juice, or laundry bleach. First cut the bottom off the bottle. Then cut two slanted sides from the bottle leaving the handle intact.

You will have a useful tool for pouring out the contents of a puddle, to use with your rainy day science projects, or for digging, scooping, and building.

You will probably find many uses for your "super scoop" on sunny days as well.

44

CUTOUT CHEER-UPS

to add color to your window

To make cheerful window cutouts to brighten your room on a dreary day you will need brightly colored construction paper, cellophane or tissue paper, white glue, scissors, and sewing thread.

With the construction paper folded in half, trace some rainy day objects such as umbrellas, raindrops, and rainbows onto the paper. Cut each one double, so you will have two exact objects. To add interest, cut out designs in your objects (rainbow stripes or colored panels in umbrellas). Cut pieces of cellophane or tissue paper large enough to cover these cutout designs.

On one of the shapes, brush white glue around the cutout and then lay cellophane or tissue pieces over it. Press until they stick. Outline the cutout with more glue (on the same side as the pasted cellophane). Then, using the second shape, sandwich the cutout over the cellophane. Press until secure.

Punch a hole near the top and hang the cutout in a sunny window.

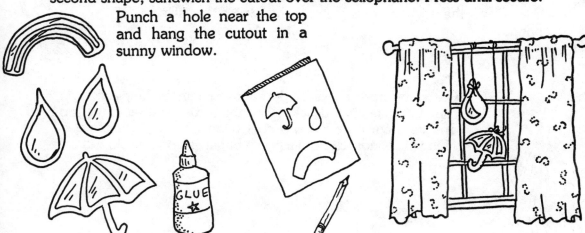

CELEBRATE THE WIND

try these wind creations

Make a weather vane, a windsock or a set of wind chimes to help you become "weather wise."

Use nylon sewing thread and string big nails onto a coat hanger and hang it on a tree branch to make wind chimes. They will provide music for your ears while they tell you a lot about the way the wind is blowing.

Make an easy weather vane that really works. Place a straight pin through the center of a drinking straw. Slit the straw and insert an arrowhead made from cardboard. Push the pin into the eraser of a pencil. Tie the pencil onto the end of a long stick. Place the stick in the ground and watch the wind change.

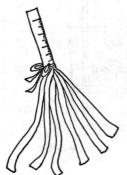

Cut strips from an old nylon shower curtain or plastic rain cape to make a windsock. Wind the strips together at the top and tie them on a ruler, a coat hanger, or a piece of rope. Hang the windsock from a porch or garden pole to blow in the wind.

RAINDROP COOKIES

there's nothing quite so nice
as the smell of spice

6 tablespoons butter
1 cup sugar
2 cups flour
1½ teaspoons baking powder
½ teaspoon salt

1 teaspoon vanilla
1 egg
1 tablespoon milk
cinnamon
sugar

Mix the butter and sugar together in a big mixing bowl. Add the egg and beat it in. Add the milk and vanilla. Sift the flour, baking powder, and salt into a small bowl. Dump this mixture into the big bowl and stir until you have a smooth dough. Break off pieces of the dough and roll into balls. Place the balls of dough on a greased cookie sheet. Mix up some cinnamon and sugar in a flat dish. Rub the bottom of a juice glass with butter. Dip the buttered glass into the cinnamon/sugar mixture and use it to flatten the balls (not too flat). When all the cookies are shaped, use your finger to press raindrops in the cookies. Use the leftover cinnamon/sugar mixture to sprinkle inside the raindrops. Bake the cookies for about ten minutes in a 375 degree oven.

This should give you 24 good fat cookies — a dozen for you and a dozen to share with some good rainy day friends.

RAINBOWS READY TO MAIL

a note that needs no envelope!

The next time you are kept inside because of rain, use the time to make some rainbow notes to send special messages to your friends.

You will need scissors, a variety of colored construction paper, and colored felt tip pens.

Cut the sheets of paper into rectangular shapes about 6" x 10". Use the felt tip pens to draw and color a rainbow in the top right hand corner of each note. Make each one different so that your friends will receive a "one-of-a-kind made-by-you note." You won't need an envelope because if you fold up the bottom of the paper about 3½" and fold down the top about 2½", you can fasten it together with a pretty sticker or a piece of tape.

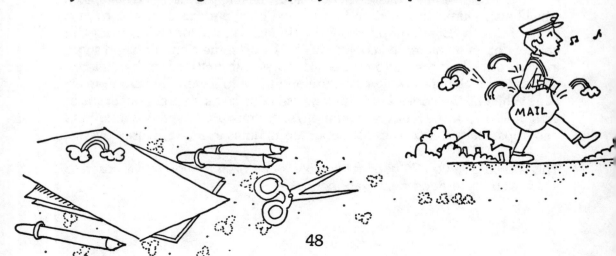

DECORATIVE DESIGNS

to make from the leftovers

For this activity you will need scissors and strips of construction paper. You are now ready to while away a rainy day making decorative designs. These borders may be used to trim scrapbooks, frame pictures, or as gift tags or place cards.

First, fold your paper in half, then into thirds. Draw any design you wish on the paper — trees, dolls, boats, or whatever you like. Next, cut out your design remembering that some part of each edge must remain uncut in order for your designs to remain linked.

Unfold it, and you will have a decorative design to make any rainy day bright and cheery. Wouldn't it be nice to make these to be used on trays for the children's wing of a hospital or for senior citizens in a nursing home?

PUT A WORD ON THE LINE

to finish up a rhyme

Find the words in the word-find puzzle on the following page to finish each of the rhymes.

1. April showers bring May _____ .

2. Rain, rain go away,
   The children want to _____ .

3. The ducks were in a huddle
   In the middle of the _____ .

4. All around the town
   The rain is coming _____ .

5. Drip, drip, drip, drop
   Please make the rain _____ .

6. That poor pet
   Is sure to get _____ .

7. The old man sadly said
   "Raindrops keep falling on my _____ ."

8. It's fun to watch the rain
   Splash on the window _____ .

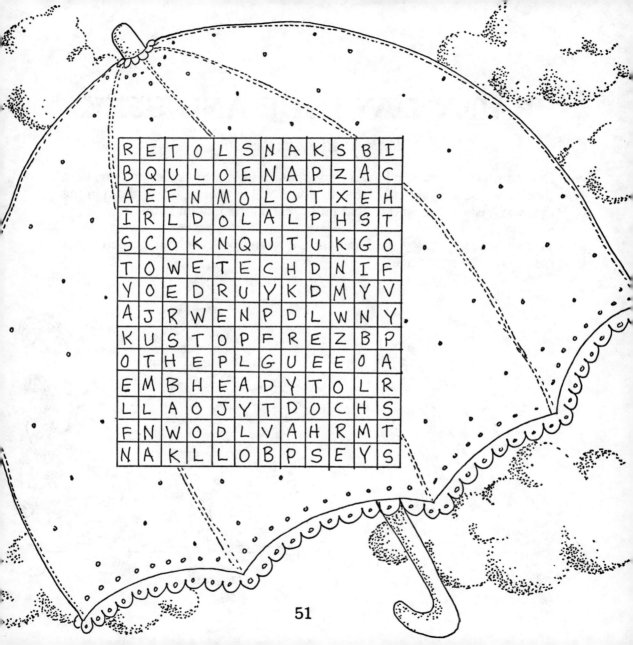

RAINY DAY HIDE AND SEEK

look carefully at this one

Draw a special rainy day fun card to amuse a friend. Select a rainy day item (boots, rainbow, raincoat, cloud) and try to hide at least ten of them in the drawing. Ask your friend to find and circle all the hidden items.

To help you get started, find and circle the ten boots we have hidden in the picture on the next page.

I WONDER WHY?

things to find out

RAINY DAY RESEARCH KIT

for times when you wonder why?

Do you know?

> … what causes a rainbow?
> … how rain clouds look and what they are called?
> … why mushrooms and toadstools spring up after a rain?
> … the average daily rainfall in your town?
> … how to study the wind to predict weather changes?

Finding answers to questions like these and enjoying the other projects in the "I Wonder Why?" section of this book will be lots easier if you have your own rainy day research kit ready to turn to. Find an old briefcase or school satchel large enough to hold reference books, notebook, sketch pad, pencils, tracing paper, paper clips, and bookmarkers. Begin to make a list of good books to use and add to it as you find new ones.

Be sure your kit has a good handle because you will want to carry it from room to room, inside and outside, and maybe to the library, the park, or a museum. Where you go to do your research will depend on how many resources you have available at home. You can have fun and learn a lot even if you have to do all of them in your own kitchen and backyard.

HOW PURE IS PURE?

can you tell the difference?

Find two glass jars exactly alike (the same size and shape). Place one of the jars outside to catch enough rainwater to almost fill it. Fill the other jar with the same amount of tap water from the sink. Place both jars side by side. Leave them overnight to see what happens. The next day check the jars to see how the water in each looks.

- Which has changed the most, the rainwater or the tap water?
- Which jar has the clearer water?
- Which jar has the most sediment at the bottom?
- Is the water temperature different in the two jars?
- Rub some water on your hands. Which feels softer?
  - What kinds of minerals or chemicals do you think there might be in the water in each jar?
  - Where does the rainwater come from?
  - Where does the tap water come from?

THE BIG COVER UP

find out some answers to those questions

Put on your gear and enjoy the rain.
Take a nature walk to try to find out . . .

What do birds do when it rains?

What makes puddles?

How do raindrops taste?

What makes the rainbow's colors?

Where do worms go when it rains?

RAIN GAUGE

a way to calculate the rainfall

Have you ever watched a television weatherman explain how barely a trace of rain has been recorded that day in your town only to glance out your window and see raindrops splattering into huge puddles right before your eyes?

How is rainfall officially recorded? In most areas a special rain gauge is used by meteorologists at the weather bureau. These gauges measure rainfall by the amount of rain that falls in one cubic inch of space.

Set up your own weather station in your backyard. First, you will need a clear, straight-sided glass bottle — an empty spice bottle or a small pickle jar will do nicely. Carefully label it with inches and quarter inches using nail polish applied with a steady hand.

Secure your bottle with cord or wire to a small board being careful to leave enough slack for easy removal. Nail or wire your rain gauge to a fence or pole in an outdoor open space. After each rainfall, measure the amount of water in your gauge. You may be surprised at just how much it does rain.

THREE WOULD RATHER BE DRY

do you know why?

One of these animals likes the rain and will not mind being "all wet." The other three would rather be dry. Find out which animal enjoys being wet and why. Then find out what the other three animals will do when the rain begins to fall.

WEATHER FORECAST

check up on the weatherman

Find a calendar with large squares for each day of the month, or make one of your own from a large sheet of drawing paper. Draw weather symbols comparable to the ones on the following page and cut them out. Code half of the symbols with a green circle and half with a red circle. Pin up the calendar in a convenient place and put the paper cutouts and a package of straight pins near by.

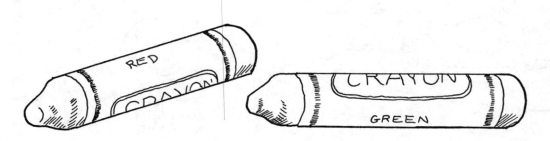

Listen to the weather forecast on the radio or television each night before you go to bed. Pin the symbol on the calendar to indicate the type of weather prediction for the next day. The next day pin on the symbol to show what the weather actually is. Use either red or green for the weatherman's predictions and the other color for the actual weather conditions. At the end of the month, count the number of squares that have two alike symbols and the number that are different. This will give you a good indication of how accurate the weatherman is.

Read the weather forecast in the daily newspaper too, to find out how closely the newspaper, radio, and television compare. Just for fun, you can add your own predictions to the lot.

SOIL CONSERVATION EXPERIMENT

learn to protect the topsoil

Only the very thin, topmost layer of our planet Earth produces all of our fruit, vegetables, grass, and trees. This topsoil is very fragile and may be washed away quite easily through misuse. Modern farmers understand how to plow furrows in their fields without damaging this precious outer layer.

Choose a rainy day to demonstrate to your family or friends how topsoil must be treated in order to conserve it. Select two large shallow pans (cookie sheets would be fine). Fill them with about two inches of soil, packed down somewhat and sloping to form a hill on one end.

With one "cookie-sheet field" you can demonstrate wasteful methods of tilling the land by digging a furrow with your finger across the top of the hill and extending long straight furrows down to the foot of the hill.

With the other field connect the top furrow with parallel trenches going back and forth across the pan until the foot of the hill is reached. This method of tilling called contour plowing resembles an unbroken coil, and protects precious topsoil.

Set your pans outside on a picnic table during the next gentle rainfall. Raise the hilled ends slightly. Place two buckets on the ground underneath to catch the draining dirt. After about five minutes, compare the amount of mud in each bucket. Your contoured field should have lost less topsoil than the straight-furrowed field.

nimbus

STUDY
THE CLOUDS

then make one of your own

stratus

Even though cloud watching from time to time is enjoyable, most of us forget a lot of what we read or hear about clouds. You probably know that cirrus clouds most often mean clear weather. Cumulus clouds may become thunder clouds. Stratus clouds spread out in flat layers often bring warnings of bad weather. Nimbus clouds are rain clouds.

Do you know how these clouds are formed?

cumulus

Here is a simple science experiment to help you understand how warm air rises to meet colder air in the sky to form clouds. These clouds gather and hold moisture until the drops get heavy enough to fall to the earth as raindrops.

1. Pour about two inches of very hot water into a glass jar and let it stand for a few minutes.
2. Darken the room or put the jar in a dark spot.
3. Put a metal tray of ice cubes over the top of the jar.
4. Shine a flashlight or a lamp toward the middle of the jar.

You will see a small cloud beginning to form in the jar.

Can you explain what causes clouds?

THERE'S MORE TO A PUDDLE

than meets the eye

After a rainstorm, stake out a nice big puddle. Take your time to investigate it thoroughly. You'll need a scoop (you'll find directions for making a nifty one on page 44) and two fat glass jars with screw-on lids. A magnifying glass will be nice if you have one, but if not, you will just need to look more carefully with your own eyes.

Look into the puddle to see how the surface of the water looks. Is it shiny like a mirror or is it wavy like the ocean? Why? Lean over very close to the puddle and try to see your own face reflected on the surface. Is your face right side up or upside down? Move around to try to get different views of yourself. They may be a bit distorted, but it will be fun all the same.

Examine the puddle closely. You may be surprised to find that your puddle has already provided a home for some small animals. If so, you will want to watch the animals for a while, try to identify them, and leave them to enjoy their wet world. Look for grass and weeds, sticks and stones, and who knows what else — you may even find a few bones! Try to find out how all these things ended up in one puddle. What will happen to all of them when the puddle drys up?

WATCH THAT PUDDLE

there's a lot to learn

Next, take your scoop and gently scoop water off the top of the puddle to half fill one jar. Then, dip all the way to the bottom of the puddle, lifting up some of the sludge at the bottom in your scoop. Half fill the other jar this way. Carry the jars inside and place them on a flat table where they can remain for a few days. Do not put the lids on the jars just yet.

Watch the jars for a day or two to see what happens. Did you scoop up any animals? What is happening to them now? What happened to the dirt and debris in the water? Has it settled to the bottom? How long did it take? How does the water in the two jars differ?

If you have a magnifying glass, place a drop of water from each jar on a piece of plastic wrap and look at them closely.

On the second day, screw the lids on the two jars and shake the water. Watch carefully to see how long it takes the dirt in each jar to settle and what happens before the water is clear again.

Isn't there more to a puddle than you thought?

THROW YOUR WEIGHT AROUND

will it sink or float

Do a little experimenting to find out why some things sink to the bottom of the puddle while others float on top. Throw a small rock into the puddle, then a big rock, then a handful of pebbles. What happens to the surface of the water each time? Why? Throw a feather, a cork, or a sponge into the puddle. What happens to the surface of the water this time? How is it different? Now pitch in a flower, a leaf, or a handful of twigs. Just for fun, try an envelope, a nail, or a small piece of soap. Why do you think some of the things float for a little while, but then sink to the bottom?

22 OTHER FUN THINGS TO DO ON A RAINY DAY

- Bake a giant gingerbread boy or girl (or buy one at a grocery store or bakery), and use this recipe to "paint" on a raincoat and boots.

  Cookie paint recipe
      1 cup sifted powdered sugar
      ¼ teaspoon salt
      ½ teaspoon vanilla
      1½ tablespoons milk or water

Blend milk in mixture to make it spread easily. Tint with yellow food coloring. "Paint" on after gingerbread is baked.

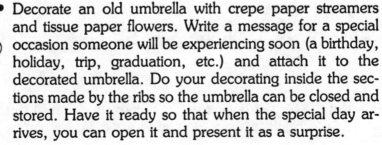

- Go to the library and look for a good book to read while you listen to the sound of rain on the roof.

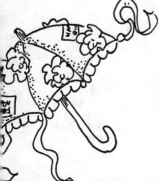

- Decorate an old umbrella with crepe paper streamers and tissue paper flowers. Write a message for a special occasion someone will be experiencing soon (a birthday, holiday, trip, graduation, etc.) and attach it to the decorated umbrella. Do your decorating inside the sections made by the ribs so the umbrella can be closed and stored. Have it ready so that when the special day arrives, you can open it and present it as a surprise.

- Find a song book and look for a rainy day song to learn to sing, or find a record that you can sing along with.

- Pretend that you are the weather reporter for your town's newspaper. Write a weather report for the entire day, including time of day, clouds, temperature, and rainfall. (Remember, a report tells what really happened while a forecast predicts what may happen.)

- Take someone younger than you for a walk in the rain and point out interesting things along the way. Since he or she is younger than you, you will want to be sure proper clothing is worn, and ask permission for the rain walk from the adult in charge.

- See how many new words you can make out of the word RAINBOW. Try for at least 20.

- Put the biggest bucket you can carry (full that is) outside to catch rainwater to use to water house plants.

• Look up rain forests in an encyclopedia or other reference book, then locate some on a globe or world map.

• Make yourself a pair of rose colored glasses to look through on the gloomy day. Cut the eye glasses from heavy cardboard and paste rose colored cellophane paper in for the lenses. (If you don't have rose colored cellophane, use clear plastic wrap and "just pretend" it is rose.) Look through the glasses and think cheerful thoughts.

• Make up a television commercial for a brand new type of umbrella made from material guaranteed to last a lifetime and include a button for a speaker that beeps, "I'm a poor, little lost umbrella, please return me to my owner at (owner's address)."

• Make a list of words that rhyme with rain. Then rhyme around with shower, splash, puddle, and drip. When your lists are finished, use them to make rainy day poems.

• Play a rainy day version of the old-fashioned game of Buzz. All players sit in a circle. Players take turns counting off numbers in turn. When seven is reached, that player must say "It isn't raining on me" instead of seven. When he fails to do so and says seven, he is out of the game. The game continues until only one player is left to be declared the winner.

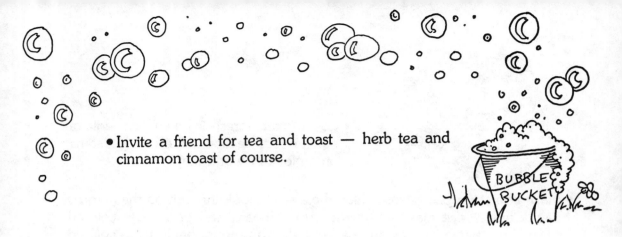

• Invite a friend for tea and toast — herb tea and cinnamon toast of course.

• Put a pail outside to "catch a pail of rainwater." Bring the pail inside and pour three or four tablespoons of cooking oil or baby oil on top. What happens? Now shake the pail from side to side and observe the water. Stir the oil and water together with a spoon, then set it back on the table for a few minutes. What happens now? What does this science experiment prove?

• And while you have your pail out, empty the pail and dry it well. Set it outside to "catch another pail of water." Use liquid dishwashing detergent mixed with a little glycerin to make bubble mix supreme. Actually, if you don't have the glycerin, the liquid detergent will work by itself. The glycerin just makes stronger bubbles. Add a little food coloring if you want more colors. Get any of these (all of them if you can) to use to blow your rainy day bubbles. It's fun to see the different sizes and shapes you can get. (Try old spools, drinking straws, jar rings, big paper clips, a funnel, small strainers, slotted kitchen spoons, tops from spice shakers (ones with tiny holes), and a key ring with a metal loop.)

- Design a rain suit to keep your teacher dry from head to toe. Think about the style and kind of material the teacher likes, and make "a suit sure to suit."

- Make up some rainy day exercises to keep your body in shape. Stretch, swing, sway, kneel, lie flat, up and down, back and forth, head and feet, arms and legs, toes and torso, move all your body parts. Experiment and practice until you have a set of exercises just right for a rainy day. Then, find a favorite record or tape and set your exercises to music.

- Be a word painter and choose one of the words below to write over and over to show the shape of the word. (Try umbrella, boot, raindrop, and puddle.)

- Make an emergency rain suit for yourself out of a plastic dress bag and a brown paper bag. Cut a hole for your head and arms in the plastic bag, and use the brown paper bag for a hat.

• There is nothing your mother would less like to have than a muddy hand print on her wall — right? Wrong! Wrong that is if you make your hand print outdoors on a piece of cardboard. Do it just after the rain stops while the mud is still just right for making hand prints. Collect your cardboard, make your hand print, and leave your hand print to dry in the sun. Later, trim around the cardboard to get the size you want. Cover the trimmed cardboard with clear plastic wrap. Then, frame it and give it to mother as a gift. Be sure to write the date on the print because it is apt to become a treasured keepsake. Everyone will be so glad to remember that all that mud was outside not inside the house.

• Read the story of Noah and the ark. Try to imagine what a rain that lasted 40 days and 40 nights would be like. According to the story, Noah was told to fill the ark with a pair of each animal on Earth, male and female. Can you imagine what a project this must have been for Noah? Did you know that animals not only have names for their particular species, but also are named according to whether they are male or female? Of course you recognize a horse when you see one, but if you want to be more specific in your identification of this animal, you could refer to a female horse as a mare and a male horse as a stallion. See if you can make a list of some other animal pairs.